SHANGHAI

主编：李　新

D1729773

上海人民美術出版社

目录 | CONTENTS

上海，简称沪，亦称申。地处长江三角洲平原东端，面积6000平方公里，人口约1700万。是我国四大直辖市之一，最大的城市和经济中心，也是国际大都市之一。

不知是日新月异吸引海纳百川，还是海纳百川促成日新月异，上海的魅力绵延百载，与日俱增——

上海，一座色彩斑斓的城市。清晨，红润的朝霞为城市梳妆；傍晚，光灿的夕阳为浦江披金。日间，车流人海生生不息，勾画着五彩缤纷的市井抽象图；夜幕，各色灯光熠熠生辉，镶嵌着晶莹剔透的"东方明珠"。

上海，一座活力四射的城市。江河，大桥飞跃、隧道潜穿，谱写世纪精彩；路旁，商厦林立、楼群攀升，烘托都市华章。港口，巨轮每天吞吐数万标箱，汽笛欢唱；街心，绿地每天演绎自然清新、鸟语花香。

上海，一座风尚浪漫的城市。发祥，在以豫园为中心的"老城厢"会馆名园、庙观教堂间飘逸江南街市的风情；开埠，在以外滩为一线的"万国建筑"和"十里洋场"弥漫"东方巴黎"的风韵。商业，在豪华典雅的店堂、多姿多彩的节日里，显示前卫新潮的国际时尚；文化，在传统和现代、东方与西方、经典与浪漫、高雅与流行的交织中，创造完美卓越的时代篇章。

上海，这个人口仅占全国1%、土地面积占全国0.06%的城市，完成的工业总产值占全国的1/12，港口货物吞吐量占全国的1/10，口岸进出口商品总额占全国的1/8，财政收入占全国的1/8，并在改革开放、产业升级、科技创新等方面发挥着示范、辐射和带动作用。

充满魅力的上海，让人品味、让人陶醉……

Preface

....Located in the east end of Yangtze River delta plain, Shanghai is one of the four municipalities directly under the Central Government, with an area of 6,000 square kilometers, and an approximate population of 17,000,000. Being a metropolitan, the economic center and the largest city in China, Shanghai is abbreviated as Hu, or Shen.

....Shanghai's glamour increases each day...

....Shanghai, a colorful city. The rosy dawn, golden dusk, multicolored day, brilliant night, plus the glorious Oriental Pearl TV Power, comprise a vivid picture.

....Shanghai, a dynamic city. The bridges, tunnels, stores, high-rises, vessels, bird chirps, flowers, green belts, show the vitality of Shanghai.

....Shanghai, a fashionable and romantic city. Traditional culture is expressed in old city areas, temples, gardens; the mien of "oriental Paris" is showed on the world architectures and foreign markets; the commerce booms in elegant stores and on happy festivals — a chapter of excellence and perfection, of east meeting west, old meeting new has been written.

....Shanghai, whose population only takes percentage of 1% in China, land 0.06%, has produced China's 1/12 GDP, 1/8 trade volume, 1/8 financial revenues, and can handle China's 1/10 cargo. It also plays a crucial and leading role in reform and opening-up, industry upgrade, technological breakthroughs.

....Glamorous Shanghai is of taste and fascination.

19 世纪 80 年代 | 20 世纪 20 年代
1880s | 1920s

20 世纪 30 年代 | 20 世纪 40 年代

1930s | 1940s

都市新景

..................................上海的每一天都在变化，上海的新景观令人目不暇接。

..................................建筑：商务大厦日益刷新城市标高，公共设施每每塑造现代化城市标志，在浦江两岸交相辉映。

..................................交通：高架道路在楼林间隙蜿蜒，大桥不断飞跨浦江超越世界纪录，地铁编织密集地下网络连通各个角落。

..................................社区：商业与居住交错并进，环境人性化、生态化、艺术化，徐家汇、五角场等城市副中心扩展繁荣，市郊"一城九镇"初露端倪。

..................................绿地：多功能的植被与水系遍布，形成都市绿色景观带，营造人与自然的温馨。

..................................林林总总的新景观会令你：在"东方明珠"感叹都市奇迹；在滨江大道抒发浪漫情怀；在"新天地"眷顾昔日氛围；在延中绿地流连翠色沁香。

..................................上海，这座东方大都市每一天都在发展，每一天都在等待你去发现令人激动不已的新视角。

☐ New Landscape in Metropolitan

....Countless new landscapes show up in the ever changing Shanghai.

....Architecture: Commercial buildings become higher and higher, and the public facilities have always been symbols of modern city.

....Traffic: City viaducts, metro network, bridges over the Huangpu River, are all achievements of traffic construction.

....Communities: The communities combine residential and business functions, with ecological and artistic environment. Sub-centers, like Xujiahui and Wujiaochang, extend and flourish. "One City Nine Towns" in the suburbs, is in the initial stage of development.

....Green belts: The multi-functional vegetation and rivers abound, making green urban landscape, and bringing comfort to human.

....We have just listed some achievements above. You will see with your own eyes, the marvelous "Oriental Pearl TV Tower", the romantic "Riverside Avenue", the yesterday-meeting-today "Xintaindi", and the beautiful Yanzhong green belt.

....Shanghai is developing each day, and is waiting for you to find exiting new things.

东方明珠
The Oriental Pearl TV
Tower

1 3

东方明珠塔建成于 1994 年 10 月 1 日，整座塔高为 468 米。主体由晶莹夺目的圆球构成，寓予"大珠小珠落玉盘"的诗意。

Finished in October 1st, 1994,the totally 468-meters-high Oriental Pearl TV Tower comprises several hemispheres, implying "big and small pearls".

浦江风景线
Sightseeing along the
Huang Pu River

14
15

浦西外滩"万国建筑博览"建筑群, 浦东陆家嘴现代高楼群、绿色滨江大道, 使浦江两岸构成了一条独特的都市风景线。

A beautiful sight along the Huangpu River: the museum of international architecture in the bund, Puxi; the skyscrapers in Lujiazui, Pudong Area; and the green Riverside Avenue along the bund.

陆家嘴风采
Lujiazui

16 17

陆家嘴金融贸易区聚集了150多家中外金融机构、4000多家贸易公司以及300多家跨国公司，日益凸显其核心功能区的作用。

The location has attracted over 150 Chinese and foreign financial institutions, over 4,000 trade companies, and over 300 MNCs, which highlights the Lujiazui Finance and Trade Zone as a core area.

科技腾飞
Technology Boom

18
19

上海科技馆是一座大型的综合性科技馆，建筑面积9.8万平方米，坐落于浦东世纪公园之侧。翔升的造型恰似上海科技腾飞，又寓含科技发展的曲折进程。

Large and comprehensive, the Shanghai Science and Technology Museum is located near Century Park in Pudong, covering a floor area of 98,000 square meters. The flying shapes resemble Shanghai's rapid development of technology, as well as implying the winding course of technological development.

陆家嘴夜色
Nocturnal Scene of
Lujiazui

昔日浦东荒凉的农田，现在已经建设成为"东方曼哈顿"，夜间华灯辉映，与对岸的外滩万国建筑夜景遥相竞辉，成为都市旅游的热点。

The once desolate farmland has been changed into 'oriental Manhattan', and a tourist attraction. In the night, the brilliant lights form a beautiful nocturnal scene, which can rival the night scene of the Bund across the river.

日晷 耀 东方
The Sundial

21

位于上海浦东世纪大道的景观雕塑设计"东方之光"(日晷)，垂直高度达 20 米，上小下大的椭圆形晷盘也象征着地球，晷针穿过的中点代表中国。

The scenic sculpture—the Oriental Light is erected at Century Avenue, Pudong, with 20 meters of height, and with the oval sundial plate symbolizing the Earth, and the center of the Sundial pin symbolizing China.

神速磁浮
The Miraculously
Speedy Maglev

22

新建在浦东的世界首条用于商业营运的磁悬浮列车线路，时速可达 400 多公里。
The newly built Maglev, with the speed at 400 kilometers per hour, is the first commercial Maglev in the world.

世纪公园
Century Park

23

世纪公园位于上海市浦东新区行政文化中心,是上海内环线中心区域内最大的富有自然特征的生态型城市公园。

Located at the Administration and Culture Center of Pudong New Area, Century Park is the biggest natural park within the inner-ring downtown area.

缤纷外滩 The Bund	**24**	节日夜晚的外滩上空，璀璨多姿的烟花绽放，将外滩妆点得更加绚丽迷人。 On festivals, colorful fireworks have popped up the sky, adding to the Bund's charm.
人民广场中心广场 The Heart of People's Square	**25**	位于人民大道南侧，博物馆北侧，面积3844平方米，广场的中央是320平方米的圆形音乐喷水池，为三层9级下沉式。喷水池中央凸现上海的版图，喷水池四周是4座紫铜花坛。 South of People's Avenue, and north of Shanghai Museum, the square occupies an area of 3,844 square kilometers. In the center of the square, is a three-floor sinking round music fountain which covers an area of 320 square meters. In the center of the fountain, protrudes Shanghai map; and around it, are four red copper flower beds.

人民广场
People's Square

26
27

位于上海市中心，曾经是号称远东第一的"上海跑马厅"，现在是上海最大的公共广场，总面积约14万平方米。上海的市政府大厦、博物馆、大剧院、城市规划展示馆均坐落于此。

Located at the center of Shanghai, the once acclaimed No. 1 racecourse in Far East, is now the largest public square in Shanghai, covering an area of 140,000 square meters. Shanghai Municipal Building, Shanghai Museum, Shanghai Grand Theater and Shanghai Urban Planning Exhibition Center all stand here.

南浦大桥
Nanpu Bridge

28

于1991年12月1日竣工通车，总长8346米，主桥长846米，跨径423米，通航净高46米，桥下可通行5.5万吨巨轮。它是目前世界上第四大双塔双索面斜拉桥，呈"H"形的主桥塔高150米。游人可乘坐电梯到达主桥，一览浦江两岸无限风光。南浦大桥是黄浦江的第一座大桥，宛如一条巨龙横卧浦江之上，使上海人圆了"一桥飞架浦江"的梦想。

Opened to traffic on December, 1st, 1991, Nanpu Bridge is totally 8,346 meters in length, 423 meters in span, and 46 meters in navigation clear height. 55,000 tons vessels are able to navigate under the bridge. The fourth largest suspension bridge in the world, its H-shaped main tower is 150 meters in height. Nanpu Bridge, being the first bridge over the Huangpu River, has realized Shanghai people's dream of crossing the river. Tourists can take an elevator to the main bridge to appreciate beautiful scenery along Huangpu River.

卢浦大桥 Lupu Bridge	**29**	2003 年建成通车，全长 750 米，采用中承式钢拱梁全焊接系杆揽结构体系，主跨 550 米，矢高 100 米，为世界第一跨度的拱桥，跨度比排名第二的美国西弗吉尼亚大桥还长 32 米。 Lupu Bridge, opened to traffic in 2003, is totally 750 meters in length, 550 meters in span, 100 meters in arrow height. It is the longest steel arc bridge in the world, and is 32 meters longer than the American West Virginia Bridge.
"申"字高架道路 City Viaduct	**30**	上海城市道路建设日新月异，由内环高架路、南北高架路和延安路高架组成的高架线路形成"申"字形贯通市中心。 Urban roads construction in Shanghai develops at leaps and bounds. The viaduct network comprises inner-ring viaduct, north-south viaduct and Yan'an road viaduct.
静安南京路 Nanjing Road in Jing'an Area	**31**	在这里，有著名的上海展览中心、上海商城、各国领事馆、银行、跨国企业、国际级酒店、商务中心和高级餐厅云集，堪称黄金地段。 Famous Shanghai Exhibition Center, Shanghai Shopping Mall are there. Nanjing Road is also home to many consulates, banks, MNCs, international hotels, commercial centers, and first-class restaurants. The location is prime.

31

时尚之都

上海，是交汇国际时尚的前沿，中国时尚引领世界潮流之地。

上海的时尚是历史性的，在20世纪上叶，就已是屈指可数的世界时尚中心之一。东方巴黎的魅力，堪称风华绝代。

上海的时尚是全方位的，不仅是打扮的时尚，更有审美、消费、文化的时尚。

南京路——演绎商业的时尚。国际著名时尚品牌都抢先在这里"登陆"。

新天地——回顾记忆的时尚。石库门包裹着时尚的特质，激发怀旧的兴奋。

衡山路——流动休闲的时尚。各种生活方式在这里擦出时尚的火花，向四处辐射。

广场文化——传递娱乐的时尚。世界顶尖优秀文化首选这里上演，播撒激情与浪漫、绚烂与经典的时尚。

上海国际时尚之都的精彩魅力，就在这街头弄里诞生、延伸。

☐ A capital of vogue

....Shanghai is the fashion leader in China.

....Shanghai has long been a fashion center. Dating back to the early 20th century, Shanghai had been among the few fashion centers in the world. The glamour of oriental Paris could not be rivaled.

....Shanghai fashion not only means dresses, but also taste, consumption and culture.

....Nanjing Road— a commercial fashion center on which top international brands all thrive to stage.

....Xintiandi—a fashion center of old-meeting-new. Old and new, yesterday and today meet here.

....Hengshan Road— a fashionable leisure center. Various lifestyle are shown here.

....Square culture— entertainment fashion. It is a place for world-class cultural performance.

....The glamour of fashion capital can be seen in the streets and lanes.

南京路步行街 Nanjing Rd. Pedestrian Street	**36**	是上海最热闹最繁华的商业大街，被誉为"中华商业第一街"。在这里，每天的人流达到上百万人次。 Praised as "The No. 1 commercial street in China", it is the most bustling and flourishing commercial street in Shanghai, where the flow of people reaches over 1 million people every day.
南京路步行街 Nanjing Rd. Pedestrian Street	**37**	这里，汇集了数百家现代化商厦、中华老字号商店及名特产品商店，是我国最大的零售商品集散地和商业信息总汇。 It is the information hub and the largest retail hub in China where hundreds of modern shopping malls, China's old name shops and special products shops assemble.

时尚新天地 Fashionable Xintiandi		老房子，新内涵。建国中路"8 号桥"汇聚国内外创意专业团队。 Old houses have new meanings. "Eighth Bridge", a fashion centre on Jianguo Central Road gathers creative idea teams both at home and abroad.
品位新天地 Tasteful Xintaindi		上海新天地让中外游客领略上海历史文化和现代生活形态，新天地也是具文化品位的本地市民和外籍人士的聚会场所。 Xintiandi is the best place for tourists to appreciate Shanghai's history, culture and modern life style, and also for foreigners and local residents with good taste to gather.

经典新天地
Classic Xintiandi

43

"新天地"在青砖步道、清水砖墙、乌漆的大门、窄窄弄堂之间，演出了一幕精致而高贵的现代生活。

Among brick sidewalks, brick walls, painted doors and narrow lanes, the graceful and elegant modern life is revealed in "Xintiandi".

多元文化
Diversified culture

44

上海是一个兼容海内外、传统与现代文化的海派文化城市，各类文化娱乐生活丰富多彩。
Shanghai, a city absorbing domestic and foreign, modern and traditional culture, has plentiful and various kinds of cultural and recreational activities.

广场文化
Square Culture

45

上海的广场文化活动云集影视歌明星，不仅充实着各类节日，还深入到各个社区角落。
Celebrities' frequently showing up in cultural activities in Shanghai's square livens up festivals, and transmits culture to every corner of the communities.

时尚消费
Fashion consumption

46

各类国际品牌专卖商店遍布上海的各个商业圈，引领市民的时尚消费理念。
Top international brands, which can be seen in every commercial circle in Shanghai, leads citizens' concepts of fashion and consumption.

绿拥晶莹
Green Belt and Buildings

47

闹市中心郁郁葱葱的绿地簇拥着在夜空中晶莹透亮的大厦。
Buildings cluster around lush green belt ,the former being crystal and bright in the night.

正大广场
Zhengda Plaza

是上海又一新的时尚潮流的先驱和全新商业标志，汇集了久负盛名的中外品牌、环球美食及各式娱乐，每天吸引了数以万计的中外顾客。

A fashion leader and a brand-new commercial symbol, it is home to well-renowned brands, global cuisine and various kinds of entertainment, attracting hundreds of thousands of customers home and abroad.

文化名城

上海，是历史文化名城，是中国近现代史的"缩影"。

这里，宋代就有了"上海镇"，元朝置上海县；明代，更是成为全国纺织业和手工业的中心；清朝，成为全国最大的贸易港口和漕粮运输中心，被誉为江海之通津，东南之都会。

这里，鸦片战争后，许多重大的历史事件和革命活动在这里发生并影响全国。历史名流的足迹散落在上海各处的不同住宅建筑里，藏蕴着一段段耐人寻味的往事。

这里，宗教文化底蕴深厚。有历史最悠久、规模最大的千年名刹龙华寺，以供奉大型玉石坐像而闻名中外的玉佛寺，现存最古的松江清真寺，屹立于佘山顶上、宛如中世纪欧洲古城堡的圣母大教堂……

这里，"万国建筑博览"、当代文化标志性建筑会令您流连忘返。

☐ Renowned Cultural City

....Shanghai, a city famous for its history and culture, is the condensation of modern and contemporary Chinese history.

....It started from "Shanghai Town" in Song Dynasty, and was established as "Shanghai County" in Yuan Dynasty, and developed into the center of Chinese textile and handicraft industry in Ming Dynasty, and became the biggest trade port and grain transporting hub of China in Qing Dynasty. It was renowned as connection of rivers and seas, and the capital in Southeast China.

....It was where many major historical events and revolutions took place after Opium War, influencing the whole China. The anecdotes of historical celebrities can be traced in the residential architectures scattered in Shanghai.

....It had profound religion culture. There were the oldest and biggest ancient Longhua Temple, Jade Buddha Temple famous for its jade seated stature of Buddha, and the oldest mosque in China—The Songjiang Mosque, and the castle-like Mary Virgin Cathedrale on top of Sheshan.

....The museum of world architectures and the modern landmark architecture are great tourist attractions.

上海博物馆
Shanghai Museum

54

是一座大型的中国古代艺术博物馆，馆藏珍贵文物 12 万件，其中尤以青铜器、陶瓷器、书法、绘画为特色。藏品之丰富、质量之精湛，在国内外享有盛誉。

A large museum exhibiting Chinese ancient arts, it has collected 120,000 pieces precious cultural relics, among which bronze wares, china, calligraphy and paintings are features. It is famous for its rich collection and high quality exhibits.

上海博物馆
Shanghai Museum

55

是一座方体基座与圆形出挑相结合的建筑，造型具有中国"天圆地方"的寓意。它既有中国传统建筑之基座、台阶的形意，又有园林绿化的东方格调，体现了现代科技和时代精神。

The architectural style of the museum is a prominent circle based on square foundation, referring to "the round sky and the square earth". Combining the shapes of Chinese bases and steps, and the style of eastern garden greening, it embodies modern technology and the spirit of time.

建筑博览 Museum of architecture	**56**	上海外滩的许多建筑物上都还有古希腊文化的影子。 Ancient Greek culture still can be found on many architectures in the Bund.
外滩经典 The classic architecture on the Bund	**57**	外滩许多建筑带有欧洲文艺复兴时期巴洛克式风格，这是曾被英国人称为"从苏伊士运河到远东白令海峡的一座最讲究的建筑"。 Many architectures in the Bund are in the style of Baroque of European Renaissance, and this one is the British called "the most elaborate architecture from Suez Canal to Bering Strait in Far East".

外滩原海关大楼
The Former Custom-
house on the Bund

57

建于1927年，建筑风格体现出欧洲古典建筑和近代建筑相结合的文化内涵。
Completed in 1927, its architectural style combines European classicism and modern styles.

中山东一路10-12
号

10-12 Zhongshan No.
1 Rd. (E)

58
59

是外滩大楼群建筑中最显眼的一幢大楼，建于1925年。曾是汇丰银行、上海市政府的所在地，现在是浦东发展银行的所在地。

Completed in 1925, it's the most conspicuous building in Bund's architectures, being the former place of HSBC and Shanghai municipal government, it is now the place of Pudong Development Bank.

"世纪壁画" "Century Fresco"	**60**	彩色马赛克镶嵌组成的大型"世纪壁画"，是原汇丰银行大厅内装饰的重要组成部分，壁画表现了三层内容：穹顶中心的太阳神图案；12 星座图；汇丰银行分布在世界各地的城市图案并分别以自由女神等 8 位天神为象征。 The large "century fresco", made up by colored mosaic, was an import part of interior decoration of former HSBC hall, which was composed of three parts: Titan picture in dome center, 12 constellation charts, and the city icon where HSBC braches exist, symbolized by gods respectively such as the goddess of liberty.
外滩 27 号怡和洋行大楼 27 the Bund, Jardine Chatered Building	**61**	始建于 1920 年，竣工于 1922 年 11 月。外观为仿英国复古主义派建筑风格，钢筋混凝土框架结构。 The construction began in 1920 and finished in November 1922. The building was of reinforced concrete framework, and after British ancient style.

豫 园
Yu Garden

62
63

始建于嘉靖、万历年间，原是明代四川布政使上海人潘允端为了侍奉他的父亲——明嘉靖年间的尚书潘恩而建造的私人园林，取"豫悦老亲"之意，距今已有400余年历史。

With a history of more than 400 years, it was founded during the reign of Emperor Jiajing and Wanli in the Ming Dynasty, by Shanghainese Pan Yunduan, a Buzhengshi of Sichuan, to please his father Pan En—a minister during the reign of Emperor Jiajing. That is why he called this garden "Yuyuan"—because "yu" in Chinese means "peace and health".

九曲桥湖心亭
Jiuquqiao and lake-center pavilion

64

为园中著名胜景。豫园是著名的江南古典园林，可分成六大景区，每个景区都有其独特的景色。

They are famous scenic spots in Yu Garden, the latter being famous classic garden in Jiangnan, (areas south of the lower reaches of the Yangtze River, including southern Jiangsu and Anhui provinces and northern Zhejiang Province), and can be divided into six sections. Each section has its own scenery.

豫园和煦堂
Sunshine Hall in Yu
Garden

65

堂呈方形，面山背水，以"和煦融融"得名。

This square hall lies against a pond and faces the artificial landscape. It is a good place to bask in the sun.

豫园玉华堂
Yu Hua Tang in Yu Garden

66

是主人的书房。玉华堂三字为文徵明之墨宝，堂内是典雅的明代书房摆设，书案、画案、靠椅、躺椅等都是明代紫檀木家具的珍品。

Yu Hua Tang was once the master's study, furnished in typical style of Ming Dynasty. The writing desk,painting desk,armchair,deck chair are all treasures of rosewood furniture in Ming Dynasty. The name was written by Wen Zhengming.

"穿云龙墙"
"Chuan Yun Long Wall"

67

豫园从鱼禾榭到万花楼一带，有游廊、溪流、山石等景物，多庭院小景，极具玩味。此亦为园中佳景。

This is among the abundant and tasteful corridors, streams, stones in the section from Yuhe Pavilion to Flower House.

西藏路沐恩堂 Mu'en Church on Xizang Rd.	**68**	原建于1887年汉口路云南路，为当时美国流行的学院哥特式建筑。1930年重建于西藏路。 It was originally built at the connecting point of Yunnan Rd. and Hankou Rd., in 1887, and in the style of college Gothic, which was then popular in America. The reconstruction took place in 1930, and the address moved to Xizang Rd.
徐家汇教堂内景 Interior view of Xujiahui Church	**69**	该堂内部呈十字形，纵向形成前厅、中厅、后厅，后厅之上是唱诗楼；横向形成南北两厢。 In the crisscross church, on the vertical axis are there lobby, middle hall, and rear hall, above which is choir room, and on the horizontal axis are there north and south wings.

董家渡天主教堂
Dongjiadu Cathedral

70

1847 年建，1853 年落成，是当时中国第一座天主教座堂。建筑为文艺复兴时期的巴洛克风格。

As the first Catholic church in China, it was built from 1847 to 1853, in baroque style.

徐家汇天主教堂
Xujiahui Cathedral

71

1910 年建成，帮幛建筑红土砖墙，高度为 56.6 米。圣像雕塑和尖顶钟楼双塔，俨然透着法国哥德式建筑艺术的神秘与庄重。

The 56.6-meter-high Xujiahui Cathedral was built in 1910 with red bricks. The sculpture of the saints and twin red brick spires represent the mystery and solemnity of French Gothic architecture.

钟楼
Bell Tower

72

位于南京西路 325 号，曾是 30 年代上海十里洋场的跑马总会，后又为上海博物馆、上海图书馆馆址，现为上海美术馆，已成为上海标志性的公益文化设施之一。

Located at 325, Nanjing Rd.(W), it was once the Horse Race Association of the foreign markets in 1930, and was then converted into Shanghai Museum, Shanghai Library, and finally into Shanghai Art Museum, as well as a landmark of public cultural facility in Shanghai.

马勒别墅
Moller Villa

73

位于现延安中路陕西南路拐角处，于 1936 年落成。传说这是依照当年花园主人马勒最宠爱的小女儿 "安徒生童话般的城堡" 梦境设计、投入巨资，历时 7 年建成的。

Set up in 1936, it was located at the corner of Yan' an Rd. (M), and Shanxi Rd. (S). Legend has it that this villa was designed with huge investment, with 7 years of construction, and with the owner's favorite youngest daughter's concept of a dreamy castle that would probably only appear in Anderson's fairy tales.

"大理石大厦"
"Marble Buildings"

74

座落于延安西路54号，始建于1924年，原是英籍犹太人嘉道里私宅。为西洋宫廷式样，外表极为壮观，内装修更为豪华，全部用意大利进口大理石装修。1953年后归中国福利会少年宫使用。

It was built in 1924, in the style of majestic and luxurious western palace, the interior decorated with Italian-imported marbles. Located at 54, Yan'an Rd. (W), it was the former residence of British Jews Jiadaoli, and is now used by Children's Palace of Chinese Welfare Association.

周公馆
Residence of Chou Enlai

74

上海思南路 73 号（原马思南路 107 号），1946 年中共代表团租下这幢三层花园别墅，作为中国共产党代表团驻沪办事处，但国民党当局不同意，后就改称为"周公馆"。

Locate at 73, Sinan Rd., (former 107 Masinan Rd.), it would have been CPC delegation's office in Shanghai but for the dissent from Kuomintang. Afterwards the name was changed to "Residence of Chou Enlai".

上海中山故居
The Former Residence of Sun Yat-Sen

75

坐落在香山路 7 号，建于 20 世纪初，是一幢二层的欧式花园住宅，建筑面积 452 平方米。是孙中山晚年工作和生活过的地方。

Located at 7, Xiangshan Rd, and completed in the early 20th century, it is a 2-storey European-style residence, with a floor area of 452 square meters. It was where Mr. Sun Yat-Sen had worked and lived late in his life.

爱神花园
Venus Garden

76

位于上海巨鹿路 675 号，现为上海作家协会所在地。1931 年建成，因庭园内普绪赫喷泉而闻名。它是近代著名实业家刘吉生故居。

Located at 675, Julu Rd., it is famous for Puxuhe fountain in the garden. Completed in 1931, being the former residence of famous modern entrepreneur—Liu Jisheng, it is now the place for Shanghai Writers Association.

汾阳路 79 号
79 Fenyang Rd.

77

该建筑 1905 年建成，是法国后期文艺复兴建筑样式的典范。原为法国公董局总董住宅，解放后曾是陈毅市长临时住所。现为上海工艺美术博物馆。

Completed in 1905, it was in the typical style of late French Renaissance. It was changed from the residence of the chief director of French Director Bureau, into temporary residence of Mayor Chen Yi after liberation, and finally into Shanghai Arts and Crafts Museum today.

多伦路历史名人街 Duolun Rd.	**78** **79**	靠近鲁迅公园的一条小街，全长仅550米，但以30多处名人故居而闻名海外。 A road near Luxun Park, with a total length of only 550 meters, it is famous for over 30 former residences of cultural celebrities.
"老电影" 咖啡馆 "Old Film" Café	**80**	坐落在多伦路上，是一幢日式三层小楼。底层吧台旁的大屏幕电视会播放老电影——遍及三四十年代国内和好莱坞的经典影片。 Located on Duolun Rd., it is a Japanese three-storey building, on the first floor of which old films−including domestic and Hollywood films in 1930s to 1940s, are shown on the big-screen television near the counter.

孔（祥熙）公馆
The Residence of Kong
(Xiangxi)

81

位于多伦路 250 号，建于 1924 年。建筑为砖木混合结构，外墙立面和内部装潢都具有伊斯兰建筑风格。

Completed in 1924, it is located in 250, Duolun Rd. The house is of mixed framework of brick and wood, and the walls and the interior decorations are all in Islamic style.

鲁迅故居
Former Residence of Luxun

82

位于山阴路 132 弄 9 号，是鲁迅 1933 年至 1936 年逝世前居住和工作的寓所。现屋内陈列着主人生前用过的珍贵物品和写作用具。

Located at 9# of 132 Shanyin Rd. it was Luxun's living and work place from 1933 to 1936 before his passing away. Exhibited in the room today are the writing tools and precious items which have been used by the owner.

鲁迅公园
Luxun Park

83

位于上海市四川北路 2288 号。1896 年始建，初为万国商团的打靶场，1922 年改为虹口公园。鲁迅生前常来此散步。1956 年 1 月，国务院决定将鲁迅墓迁入虹口公园，1989 年改名鲁迅公园。

Located at 2288 North Sichuan Rd. , Luxun Park was the former shooting range of International Business Commission. Founded in 1896, it was renamed as Hongkou Park in 1922 where Luxun would usually stroll. In January 1956, the State Council decided to move Luxun's tomb here and thus it was renamed as Luxun Park in 1989.

陈毅塑像 The Statue of Chen Yi	**84**	塑像坐北朝南，用青铜浇注，高5.6米，位于南京东路外滩。陈毅是新中国第一任上海市市长，为解放上海、建设上海立下了不朽功勋。 Facing south, the 5.6-meters-high bronze statue stands on the Bund. Chen Yi, first mayor of Shanghai after liberation, devoted himself to Shanghai's liberation and construction.
中山塑像 The Statue of Sun Yat-Sen	**85**	位于香山路7号孙中山故居园内。孙中山故居是我国民主革命的伟大先行者孙中山和他的夫人宋庆龄1918至1924年在上海的寓所。现在已辟为孙中山纪念馆。 It is erected in the former residence of Sun Yat-Sen, the latter was where Mr. Sun Yat-Sen, a great pioneer of China's revolution, and his wife Song Qingling lived between 1918 to 1924. Nowadays it has been converted into Sun Yat-Sen Memorial.

《智慧树》 Wisdom Tree	**86**

在上海图书馆"智慧广场"一侧，矗立着大型不锈钢雕塑《智慧树》。显示知识即力量的意境，创造了高雅宁静的文化气氛。

Wisdom Tree, a large stainless steel sculpture, erects besides Wisdom Square of Shanghai Library. It expresses the belief "Knowledge is power", as well as creates an atmosphere of quietness and elegance.

上海图书馆 Shanghai Library	**87**

坐落于淮海中路1555号，建筑面积8.3万平方米，拥有绿化面积1.1万平方米。整个建筑象征着历史文化积淀的坚实基础和人类知识高峰的不断攀登。

Located at 1555, Huaihai Rd. (M), it has a greening area of 11,000 square meters and a floor area of 83,000 square meters. The whole architecture symbolizes the accumulation of history and culture, and the incessant development of knowledge.

上海音乐厅
Shanghai Concert Hall

建于 1930 年，2002 年整体平移 66.46 米，坐落于延中绿地。建筑为欧洲传统风格，其自然音响之佳，既得到建筑学家的首肯，更为众多中外艺术家认同。

Completed in 1930, the whole concert hall moved 66.46 meters to the present address at Yanzhong green belt. The traditional European architecture style has been approved by architects, and the first-class sound system has been approved by artists from home and abroad.

上海大剧院
Shanghai Grand Theater

位于人民广场西北侧，建筑面积6万平方米，结构为简洁流畅的几何形造型，皇冠般的白色弧形屋顶弯翘向天际，形似聚宝盆，象征着上海吸纳世界文化艺术的博大胸怀。

Northwest of People's Square, it occupies a floor area of 60,000 square meters. The architecture is in fluent and simple style. The white arc-shaped roof stretches to the skyline like a cornucopia, symbolizing Shanghai's absorbing of world culture and arts.

上海马戏城
Shanghai Circus City

90

地处共和新路，有"中国马戏第一城"的美誉。其独特的建筑造型，显露了中华民族传统的"金珠银珠枕玉盘"的皇冠之气。 在夜幕下，马戏城既有华贵豪放之势，又有璀璨迷人之情。

Located at New Gonghe Rd., Shanghai Circus City is renowned as "The first circus city in China", whose unique shape resembles the splendid ancient Chinese crown. When night falls, the circus city looks noble and beautiful.

逸夫舞台
Yifu Theatre

91

是上海历史最为长久、最具规模的京剧演出场所，前身为天蟾舞台，曾有"远东第一大剧场"之誉。后由上海市人民政府投资，香港邵逸夫爵士等热心京剧艺术的人士捐助进行改建，并命名为逸夫舞台。

The oldest and biggest opera theater in Shanghai, Yifu Theatre, being the former Tianchan Theatre, was once praised as "The first grand theater in Far East". Then the restoration took place, with investment from Shanghai People's Government, and personages like Shao Yifu in Hongkong, who had enthusiasm for operas. Afterwards, it was renamed as Yifu Theatre.

上海昆剧
Kunqu Opera

92

明代万历间上海已有众多的家乐（家庭戏班）和民间班社。由明入清，上海昆剧相当繁盛，新的作品不断问世。近年来，上海昆剧团排练演出了近40个大型剧目和250出优秀传统小戏，经常应邀赴海外演出，均获得高度评价，被誉为"第一流剧团、第一流演出"。

As early as the reign of Emperor Wanli during Ming Dynasty, there had been numerous family theatrical troupes and civilian theatrical troupes in Shanghai. As time went on, and the dynasty changed from Ming to Qing, Kunqu Opera had undergone a flourishing period, when new works came out incessantly. In recent years, 40 plays and 250 playlets have been rehearsed. Their performances overseas received high appraises, and were praised as "first-class troupe" and "first-class performance".

上海京剧
Peking Opera in Shang-
hai

93

京剧来沪时，上海已是四海通商、八方交流的中国南方经济、文化中心，对外通商口岸。适应市场要求，融合海内外各剧种之所长，京剧海派艺术色彩缤纷。

When Peking Opera was introduced into Shanghai, the latter had been a foreign treaty port, and the economic and culture center in southern China. Responding to market demand, the Peking Opera absorbed essences of other kinds of dramas.

上海自然博物馆
Shanghai Nature Museum

位于延安东路上，是目前我国规模最大的自然博物馆之一，拥有24万多件藏品，包括古代自然博物馆动物史、古人类史、中国古代古尸、无脊动物、鱼类、两栖动物、爬行动物、鸟类、哺乳动物9个陈列室。

Located on Yan'an Rd.(E), is one of the largest nature museum in China, which boast its over 240,000 collected articles, including mammals, birds, amphibians, reptiles, fish, spineless animals, ancient Chinese corpse, ancient human history, animal history exhibited in 9 showrooms.

上海海洋水族馆
Shanghai Ocean Aquarium

位于浦东陆家嘴，120米长的海底观赏隧道是世界上最长的海底观赏隧道之一，8大观赏区展示了来自世界各大洲300余种（总数达1.4万尾）海洋水生物。

Located in Lujiazui, Pudong, its 120-meters-long seabed viewing tunnels is one of the longest seabed viewing tunnels in the world. Over 300 kinds of marine aquatic animals (14,000 in total number) are exhibited in 8 major exhibition sections.

海派风情

....上海，以海纳百川之情怀，兼容并蓄中外文化，在融合中创新、提升品位，演化为海派风情。

....衣：吸收天南海北之"杂"，创造种种惊艳霓裳；吃：集聚北派南帮之精华，开拓色、香、味的精致细腻；住：博采众长、融合中西，讲究实用、精巧温馨；行：上高架、下地铁，转车换乘，精明实惠；购：游逛老街、转遍商厦，精挑细选、讲究品质，追逐精美时尚；歇：小坐酒吧、咖吧、茶座，陷在沙发和袅袅的音乐中读书、看报、品饮，静心优雅；嬉：从弄堂游戏到现代酷舞，从民间收藏到观摩艺术，享受尽兴品味；游：尽览古今中外，精彩浪漫。

....上海，石库门风俗仍然在延续，与国际风尚的交流、融合不断在扩展，海派风情成为一种资源，为世界所青睐。

☐ Shanghai Culture

....Shanghai culture has been evolved from creation and perfection on the basis of absorbing essence from other culture.

....Clothing: The mixed style produces fantastic clothes;

Eating: Every Chinese cuisine is likely to be found here.

Living: The combination of east and west architectural style make beautiful, practical, delicate and cozy houses.

Traffic: Viaduct, metro, and buses are cost-effective.

Shopping: In old streets and shopping malls you are able to select anything you wanted.

Rest: Taking a rest in bars, cafés or teahouses, you can sit comfortably in the sofa, and read while listening to the music.

Fun: We can enjoy different activities from lane games to modern dancing, from folk collection to art appreciation.

Travel: You will have a wonderful tour in Shanghai.

....Shanghai has kept tradition as well as participated in international fashion exchange. Shanghai culture has been favored by the world.

100

和平饭店
Peace Hotel

100

坐落于中山东一路 20 号，原名沙逊大厦，建于 1929 年。建筑钢框架结构，平面呈 "A" 字形，塔楼部分高 12 层。

Set up in 1929, the Peace Hotel was formerly called Sassoon House. Located at 20, Zhongshan No.1 Rd. (E), it has a steel framework, an A-shaped plain layout, and a 12-storey block.

和平饭店老年爵士乐队
Senior Jazz Band in Peace Hotel

101

这是上海最有名的老年爵士乐队。这些 40 年代的乐师闲空了三四十年后，在垂暮之年，又回到和平饭店演奏当年上海的风情。

These musicians, who had not played for 30 or 40 years, go back to perform in Peace Hotel , in their declining years.

品尝上海饮食
Tasting Shanghai cuisine

102

品上海黄酒，尝上海特色小吃，成为到上海旅游的重要节目。
Sipping Shanghai yellow wine and tasting Shanghai snacks are of great importance in Shanghai tour.

上海城市历史发展陈列馆
Shanghai Urban And History Development Exhibition Hall

104

位于陆家嘴东方明珠广播电视塔内。在这里，"时光隧道"全方位展示有关老上海风情的种种传奇性故事。

It is located within Oriental Pearl TV Tower, Lujiazui, where the 'Time Tunnel' exhibits all the legendary tales about old Shanghai.

南京路老电车
Old Trolley on Nanjing
Rd.

电车在上海已经有将近 100 年的历史。老电车的再现，勾起人们多少对老上海风情的怀旧。

The old trolley has been around in Shanghai for nearly 100 years. Its reappearance reminds people of old Shanghai customs.

上海老街 Old Streets in Shang- hai	**106**	历史上曾名庙前大街，上海最早的一批钱庄、银楼、酒肆等便诞生在这里，成为当时最繁华的商业街之一，至今仍保留有较多的清末民初时期建筑风貌。 Formerly known as "Miao Qian(meaning in front of the temple) Rd.", it was one of the most bustling commercial streets then, where the first private banks, silverware shops, wine shops emerged. Architectures there are remaining from the period: from the end of Qing Dynasty to the beginning of the Republic of China.
石库门情结 Love of Shikumen	**107**	老上海居民对石库门的情怀及邻里亲情，在今天还是非常令人怀念和向往。 Old Shanghai residents are still reminiscent about the days when they lived in Shikumen and the love between neighbors then.

上海石库门民居
Shikumen Residences

石库门是海派文化在建筑上最鲜明的体现。
Shanghai culture is remarkably expressed in
Shikumen architecture.

上海的 "高度"
Altitude of Shanghai

114

上海市的首任形象大使、著名篮球运动员姚明在 "世界第一拱桥" 卢浦大桥正式竣工通车仪式上为 "跨桥第一跑" 活动领跑。

The first image ambassador of Shanghai—Yao Ming, the famous basketball player, leads the race on Lupu Bridge to celebrate its completion.

上 海 的 "速度"
Speed of Shanghai

115

奥运冠军刘翔在家门口夺得上海国际田径黄金大奖赛男子 110 米栏的金牌，也成为了上海形象代言人的 "新秀"。

Liu Xiang, who had won the golden prize of 110-meter hurdle in Shanghai International Athletics Gold Prix, has become a new Shanghai imge spokesperson.

黄 浦 江 F 1
摩托艇大赛
F1 boat racing
on Huangpu
River

118
119

F 1 摩托艇大奖赛正式落户上海。有
100 个国家的电视台直播和录播赛
事，8 亿多观众看到了上海外滩的美
丽风情。

F1 boat racing has formally staged in
Shanghai and is broadcasted in 100
countries through live and recorded
broadcast, allowing more than 800,000,
000 spectators to appreciate Shanghai's
beauty.

七宝老街
Qibao Old Street

120
121

七宝的老街深巷是北宋遗存的，亭
台楼榭是明清风格的，小桥流水是
江南特色的，然而透过古镇的青砖
白瓦，感受到的却是浓浓的海派韵
味。

The streets and lanes are relics remain-
ing from the Northern Song Dynasty;
the pavilions and terraces are built in
the style of Ming and Qing Dynasty;
and the little bridges and streams are
of Jiangnan features, however, the
combination of them make you feel
the soul of Shanghai culture.

浦江游船
Yachts on the Huangpu
River

122
123

波光粼粼的黄浦江上，各色盛妆的彩船形成一道流动的景观。置身其中，则尽享海派文化浪漫风情。

On the Huangpu River, the beautifully decorated yachts slowly pass by, in which you are able to fully appreciate the Shanghai culture.

浦江节日之夜
Huangpu River at Festival Nights

节日夜晚的外滩上空，璀璨多姿的烟花绽放和晶莹剔透的"万国建筑"交相辉映，将外滩妆得更加绚丽迷人。

At festival nights, the bright fireworks and brilliant architectures make the Bund more beautiful.

图书在版编目（CIP）数据

上海／上海人民美术出版社编. —上海：上海人民美术出版社，
2006.5
（魅力上海）
ISBN 7-5322-4776-7

Ⅰ.上... Ⅱ.上... Ⅲ. ①风光摄影－中国－现代－摄影集
②上海市－摄影集 Ⅳ.J424

中国版本图书馆CIP数据核字（2006）第025983号

撰 文：郭常明
摄 影：薛长命 陈康龄 陈宗亮 张文瑞 徐正魁 梁财国 陶洪兴
谢新发 郑宪章 李永刚 杨 立 沈以澄 李道铭 吴 谊
陈正宝 陈 路 郭长耀 浦杏兴 刘晓天 邵黎阳 赵天佐
水 众 程多多 晓 易 周国强 陈志民

魅力上海 —— 上海
主 编：李 新
策 划：周振德
封面题字：周慧珺
翻 译：陈 春
责任编辑：汤德伟
装帧设计：上海阿波罗文化艺术公司
技术编辑：陆尧春
出版发行：上海人民美术出版社
（上海长乐路672弄33号）
印 刷：上海质胜印刷有限公司
开 本：787×1092 1/24 5.34印张
版 次：2006年5月第1版
印 次：2006年5月第1次
印 数：0001-4250
书 号：ISBN 7-5322-4776-7/K·82
定 价：48.00元